Women's History Month
Female Scientists, Politicians and Astronauts

112 Internet Research Projects

C. Mahoney

Life is about choices...

Internet Safety

1

Do your work. Don't play around. You have an assignment to do, so focus your attention where it is supposed to be.

2

Search for answers to the questions. Don't get caught going down rabbit holes in search or weird or strange stuff.

3

Imagine that your mother is sitting on your right and your teacher is sitting on your left, watching what you're doing. What would they say to you right now? Make good choices.

Female Scientists

Marie Curie, Mae Jemison, Rosalind Franklin, Marie Maynard Daly, Lise Meitner, Katherine Johnson, Jocelyn Bell Burnell, Alice Ball, Roger Arliner Young, Dorothy Hodgkin, Margaret Collins, Chien-Shiung Wu, Patricia Bath, Ada Lovelace, Marguerite Williams, Barbara McClintock, Mary Anning, Rachel Carson, Rita Levi-Montalcini, Emmy Noether, Gertrude Elion, Vera Rubin, Grace Hopper, Gerty Cori, Sally Ride, Émilie du Châtelet, Hypatia, Hertha Ayrton, Caroline Herschel, Maria Mitchell, Mary Somerville, and Irène Curie-Joliot.

Marie Curie

Use a laptop, tablet or phone to access the internet and learn more about this female scientist.

Age:

Place of birth:

College:

Family:

Specialty:

Record several interesting things you learned about this female scientist:

_____
_____
_____
_____
_____

_____
_____
_____
_____

SOURCES:

_____
_____

Mae Jemison

Use a laptop, tablet or phone to access the internet and learn more about this female scientist.

Age:

Place of birth:

College:

Family:

Specialty:

Record several interesting things you learned about this female scientist:

1

2

3

4

SOURCES:

Rosalind Franklin

Use a laptop, tablet or phone to access the internet and learn more about this female scientist.

Age:

Place of birth:

College:

Family:

Specialty:

Record several interesting things you learned about this female scientist:

1

2

3

4

SOURCES:

Marie Maynard Daly

Use a laptop, tablet or phone to access the internet and learn more about this female scientist.

Age:

Place of birth:

College:

Family:

Specialty:

Record several interesting things you learned about this female scientist:

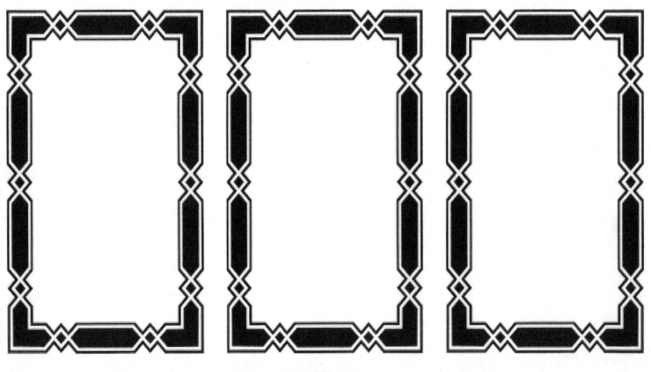

SOURCES:

_____

_____

Lise Meitner

Use a laptop, tablet or phone to access the internet and learn more about this female scientist.

Age:

Place of birth:

College:

Family:

Specialty:

Record several interesting things you learned about this female scientist:

SOURCES:

Katherine Johnson

Use a laptop, tablet or phone to access the internet and learn more about this female scientist.

Age:

Place of birth:

College:

Family:

Specialty:

Record several interesting things you learned about this female scientist:

SOURCES:

_____

_____

Jocelyn Bell Burnell

Use a laptop, tablet or phone to access the internet and learn more about this female scientist.

Age:

Place of birth:

College:

Family:

Specialty:

Record several interesting things you learned about this female scientist:

1

2

3

4

SOURCES:

_____

_____

Alice Ball

Use a laptop, tablet or phone to access the internet and learn more about this female scientist.

Age:

Place of birth:

College:

Family:

Specialty:

Record several interesting things you learned about this female scientist:

1.

2.

3.

4.

SOURCES:

_____

_____

Roger Arliner Young

Use a laptop, tablet or phone to access the internet and learn more about this female scientist.

Age:

Place of birth:

College:

Family:

Specialty:

Record several interesting things you learned about this female scientist:

1

2

3

4

SOURCES:

Dorothy Hodgkin

Use a laptop, tablet or phone to access the internet and learn more about this female scientist.

Age:

Place of birth:

College:

Family:

Specialty:

Record several interesting things you learned about this female scientist:

_____

_____

_____

_____

_____

_____

_____

_____

_____

SOURCES:

_____

_____

Margaret Collins

Use a laptop, tablet or phone to access the internet and learn more about this female scientist.

Age:

Place of birth:

College:

Family:

Specialty:

Record several interesting things you learned about this female scientist:

①

②

③

④

SOURCES:

Chien-Shiung Wu

Use a laptop, tablet or phone to access the internet and learn more about this female scientist.

Age:

Place of birth:

College:

Family:

Specialty:

Record several interesting things you learned about this female scientist:

1.

2.

3.

4.

5.

SOURCES:

_____

_____

Patricia Bath

Use a laptop, tablet or phone to access the internet and learn more about this female scientist.

Age:

Place of birth:

College:

Family:

Specialty:

Record several interesting things you learned about this female scientist:

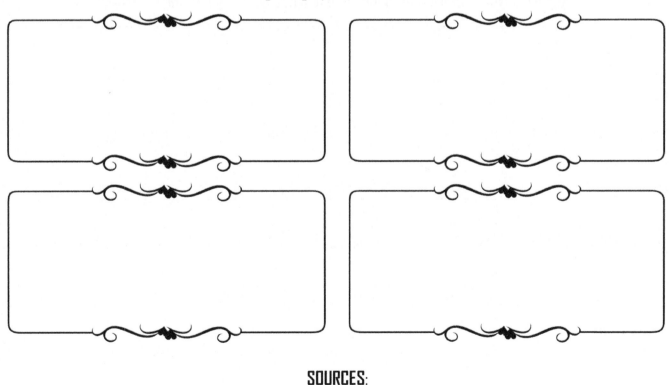

SOURCES:

_____

_____

Ada Lovelace

Use a laptop, tablet or phone to access the internet and learn more about this female scientist.

Age:

Place of birth:

College:

Family:

Specialty:

Record several interesting things you learned about this female scientist:

SOURCES:

_____

_____

Marguerite Williams

Use a laptop, tablet or phone to access the internet and learn more about this female scientist.

Age:

Place of birth:

College:

Family:

Specialty:

Record several interesting things you learned about this female scientist:

SOURCES:

_____

_____

Barbara McClintock

Use a laptop, tablet or phone to access the internet and learn more about this female scientist.

Age:

Place of birth:

College:

Family:

Specialty:

Record several interesting things you learned about this female scientist:

1._____
_____
_____
SOURCE: _____

2._____
_____
_____
SOURCE: _____

3._____
_____
_____
SOURCE: _____

Mary Anning

Use a laptop, tablet or phone to access the internet and learn more about this female scientist.

Age:

Place of birth:

College:

Family:

Specialty:

Record several interesting things you learned about this female scientist:

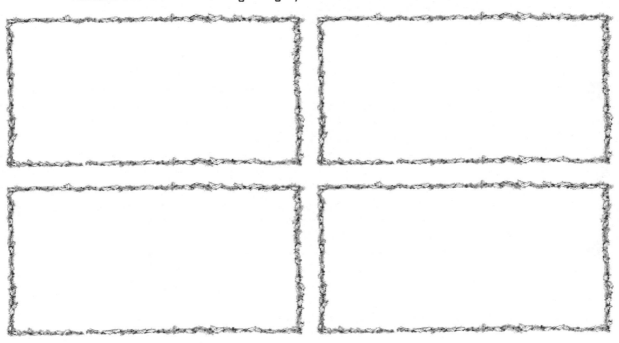

SOURCES:

_____

_____

Rachel Carson

Use a laptop, tablet or phone to access the internet and learn more about this female scientist.

Age:

Place of birth:

College:

Family:

Specialty:

Record several interesting things you learned about this female scientist:

 1

 2

 3

 4

SOURCES:

_____

_____

Rita Levi-Montalcini

Use a laptop, tablet or phone to access the internet and learn more about this female scientist.

Age:

Place of birth:

College:

Family:

Specialty:

Record several interesting things you learned about this female scientist:

SOURCES:

Emmy Noether

Use a laptop, tablet or phone to access the internet and learn more about this female scientist.

Age:

Place of birth:

College:

Family:

Specialty:

Record several interesting things you learned about this female scientist:

SOURCES:

Gertrude Elion

Use a laptop, tablet or phone to access the internet and learn more about this female scientist.

Age:

Place of birth:

College:

Family:

Specialty:

Record several interesting things you learned about this female scientist:

1

2

3

SOURCES:

Vera Rubin

Use a laptop, tablet or phone to access the internet and learn more about this female scientist.

Age:

Place of birth:

College:

Family:

Specialty:

Record several interesting things you learned about this female scientist:

1

2

3

4

SOURCES:

Grace Hopper

Use a laptop, tablet or phone to access the internet and learn more about this female scientist.

Age:

Place of birth:

College:

Family:

Specialty:

Record several interesting things you learned about this female scientist:

_____

_____

_____

_____

_____

_____

_____

_____

_____

_____

SOURCES:
_____
_____

Gerty Cori

Use a laptop, tablet or phone to access the internet and learn more about this female scientist.

Age:

Place of birth:

College:

Family:

Specialty:

Record several interesting things you learned about this female scientist:

SOURCES:

Sally Ride

Use a laptop, tablet or phone to access the internet and learn more about this female scientist.

Age:

Place of birth:

College:

Family:

Specialty:

Record several interesting things you learned about this female scientist:

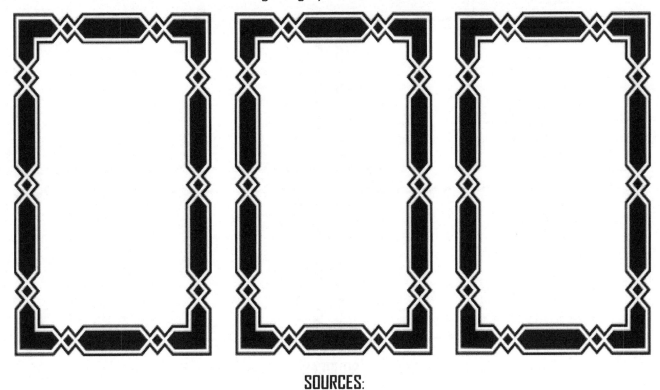

SOURCES:

_____

_____

Émilie du Châtelet

Use a laptop, tablet or phone to access the internet and learn more about this female scientist.

Age:

Place of birth:

College:

Family:

Specialty:

Record several interesting things you learned about this female scientist:

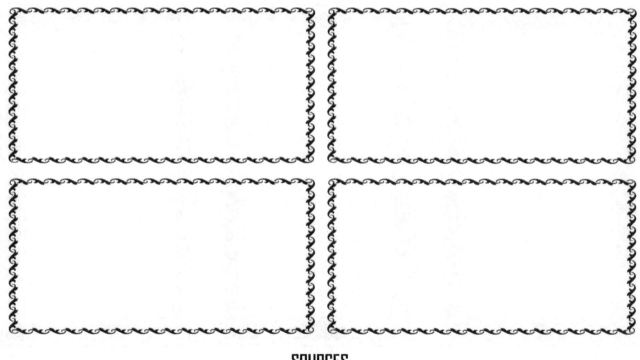

SOURCES:

_____

_____

Hypatia

Use a laptop, tablet or phone to access the internet and learn more about this female scientist.

Age:

Place of birth:

College:

Family:

Specialty:

Record several interesting things you learned about this female scientist:

1

2

3

4

SOURCES:

Hertha Ayrton

Use a laptop, tablet or phone to access the internet and learn more about this female scientist.

Age:

Place of birth:

College:

Family:

Specialty:

Record several interesting things you learned about this female scientist:

_____

_____

_____

_____

_____

_____

_____

_____

_____

_____

SOURCES:
_____
_____

Caroline Herschel

Use a laptop, tablet or phone to access the internet and learn more about this female scientist.

Age:

Place of birth:

College:

Family:

Specialty:

Record several interesting things you learned about this female scientist:

1.

2.

3.

4.

SOURCES:

Maria Mitchell

Use a laptop, tablet or phone to access the internet and learn more about this female scientist.

Age:

Place of birth:

College:

Family:

Specialty:

Record several interesting things you learned about this female scientist:

_____

_____

_____

_____

_____

_____

_____

_____

SOURCES:

_____

_____

Mary Somerville

Use a laptop, tablet or phone to access the internet and learn more about this female scientist.

Age:

Place of birth:

College:

Family:

Specialty:

Record several interesting things you learned about this female scientist:

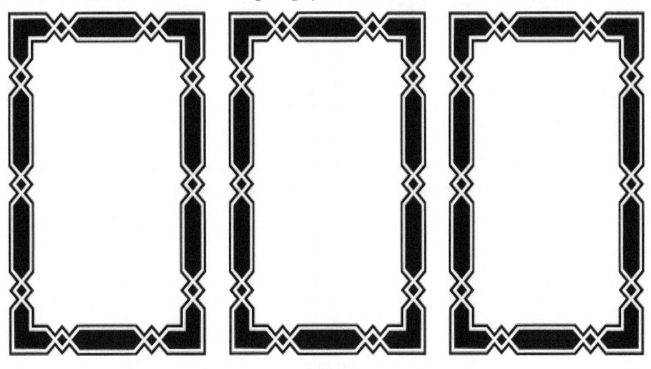

SOURCES:

_____

_____

Irène Curie-Joliot

Use a laptop, tablet or phone to access the internet and learn more about this female scientist.

Age:

Place of birth:

College:

Family:

Specialty:

Record several interesting things you learned about this female scientist:

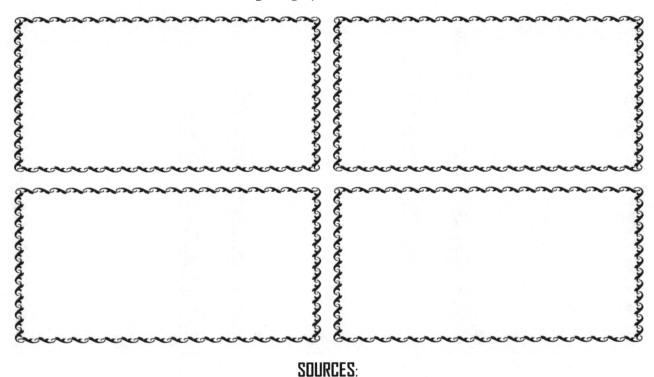

SOURCES:

_____

_____

Female Politicians

Ilhan Omar, Indira Gandhi, Alexandria Ocasio Cortez, Kamala Harris, Hillary Clinton, Nancy Pelosi, Shirley Chisholm, Angela Merkel, Stacey Abrams, Margaret Thatcher, Theresa May, Condoleezza Rice, Elizabeth Warren, Sarah Palin, Barbara Jordan, Rashida Tlaib, Mia Love, Kirsten Gillibrand, Maxine Waters, Jahana Hayes, Andrea Jenkins, Lucy McBath, Karen Bass, Loren Underwood, Carol Mosely Braun, Eleanor Holmes Norton, Donna Christian Christensen, Sheila Jackson Lee, Stacey Plaskett, Sheikh Hasini, Tsai Ing-wen, Nicola Sturgeon, Jeannette Rankin, Dalia Grybauskaite, Erna Solberg, Nikki Haley, Aung San Suu Kyi, Susan Collins, Dianne Feinstein, Ayanna Pressley, Rebecca Latimer Felton, Patty Murray, Lisa Murkowski, Victoria Woodhull, Jill Stein, Geraldine Ferraro, Michele Bachmann, Elizabeth Dole, Gabby Giffords, and Golda Meir.

ILHAN OMAR

Use a laptop, tablet or phone to access the internet and learn more about this female politician.

Age:

Place of birth:

College:

Family:

Work Place:

Record several interesting things you learned about this female politician:

_____

_____

_____

_____

_____

_____

_____

_____

_____

_____

SOURCES:

_____

_____

Indira Gandhi

Use a laptop, tablet or phone to access the internet and learn more about this female politician.

Age:

Place of birth:

College:

Family:

Work Place:

Record several interesting things you learned about this female politician:

1

2

3

4

SOURCES:

_____

_____

Alexandria Ocasio Cortez

Use a laptop, tablet or phone to access the internet and learn more about this female politician.

Age:

Place of birth:

College:

Family:

Work Place:

Record several interesting things you learned about this female politician:

1

2

3

4

SOURCES:

Kamala Harris

Use a laptop, tablet or phone to access the internet and learn more about this female politician.

Age:

Place of birth:

College:

Family:

Work Place:

Record several interesting things you learned about this female politician:

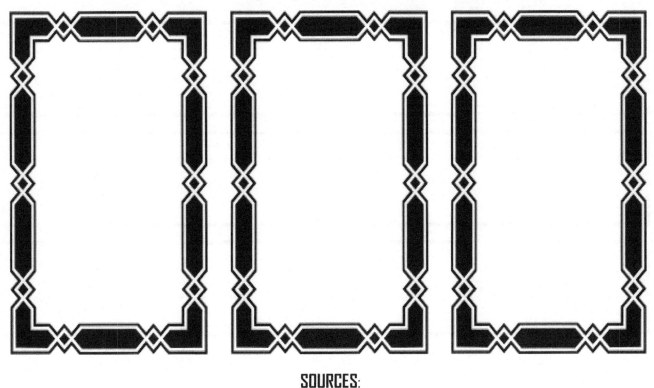

SOURCES:

_____

_____

Hillary Clinton

Use a laptop, tablet or phone to access the internet and learn more about this female politician.

Age:

Place of birth:

College:

Family:

Work Place:

Record several interesting things you learned about this female politician:

_____

_____

_____

_____

_____

_____

_____

_____

_____

SOURCES:

_____

_____

Nancy Pelosi

Use a laptop, tablet or phone to access the internet and learn more about this female politician.

Age:

Place of birth:

College:

Family:

Work Place:

Record several interesting things you learned about this female politician:

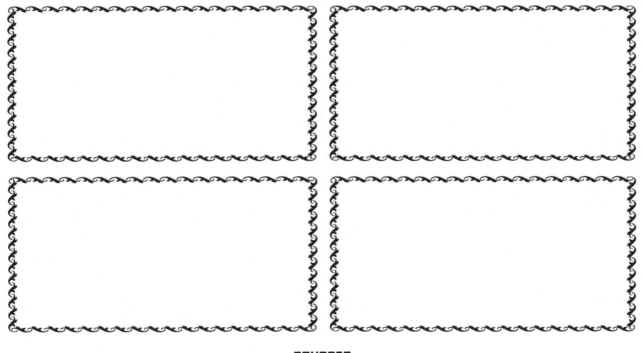

SOURCES:

_____

_____

Shirley Chisholm

Use a laptop, tablet or phone to access the internet and learn more about this female politician.

Age:

Place of birth:

College:

Family:

Work Place:

Record several interesting things you learned about this female politician:

1

2

3

4

SOURCES:

Angela Merkel

Use a laptop, tablet or phone to access the internet and learn more about this female politician.

Age:

Place of birth:

College:

Family:

Work Place:

Record several interesting things you learned about this female politician:

1

2

3

4

SOURCES:

_____

_____

Stacey Abrams

Use a laptop, tablet or phone to access the internet and learn more about this female politician.

Age:

Place of birth:

College:

Family:

Work Place:

Record several interesting things you learned about this female politician:

SOURCES:

Margaret Thatcher

Use a laptop, tablet or phone to access the internet and learn more about this female politician.

Age:

Place of birth:

College:

Family:

Work Place:

Record several interesting things you learned about this female politician:

1

2

3

4

SOURCES:

Theresa May

Use a laptop, tablet or phone to access the internet and learn more about this female politician.

Age:

Place of birth:

College:

Family:

Work Place:

Record several interesting things you learned about this female politician:

_____

_____

_____

_____

_____

_____

_____

_____

_____

SOURCES:

_____

_____

Condoleezza Rice

Use a laptop, tablet or phone to access the internet and learn more about this female politician.

Age:

Place of birth:

College:

Family:

Work Place:

Record several interesting things you learned about this female politician:

1

2

3

4

SOURCES:

Elizabeth Warren

Use a laptop, tablet or phone to access the internet and learn more about this female politician.

Age:

Place of birth:

College:

Family:

Work Place:

Record several interesting things you learned about this female politician:

1.

2.

3.

4.

5.

SOURCES:

_____

_____

Sarah Palin

Use a laptop, tablet or phone to access the internet and learn more about this female politician.

Age:

Place of birth:

College:

Family:

Work Place:

Record several interesting things you learned about this female politician:

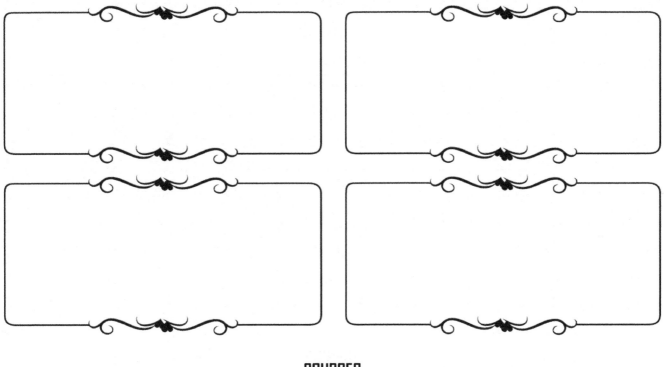

SOURCES:

_____

_____

Barbara Jordan

Use a laptop, tablet or phone to access the internet and learn more about this female politician.

Age:

Place of birth:

College:

Family:

Work Place:

Record several interesting things you learned about this female politician:

SOURCES:

Rashida Tlaib

Use a laptop, tablet or phone to access the internet and learn more about this female politician.

Age:

Place of birth:

College:

Family:

Work Place:

Record several interesting things you learned about this female politician:

SOURCES:

_____

_____

Mia Love

Use a laptop, tablet or phone to access the internet and learn more about this female politician.

Age:

Place of birth:

College:

Family:

Work Place:

Record several interesting things you learned about this female politician:

1._____
_____
_____
SOURCE: _____

2._____
_____
_____
SOURCE: _____

3._____
_____
_____
SOURCE: _____

Kirsten Gillibrand

Use a laptop, tablet or phone to access the internet and learn more about this female politician.

Age:

Place of birth:

College:

Family:

Work Place:

Record several interesting things you learned about this female politician:

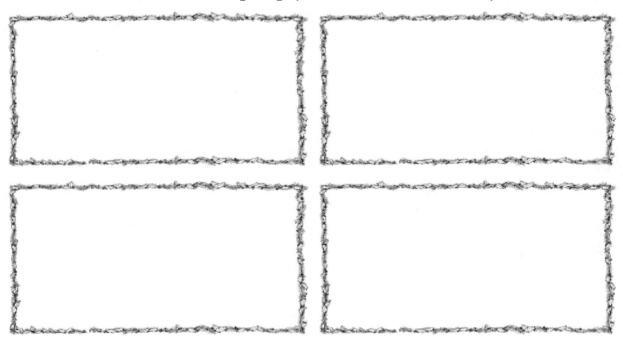

SOURCES:

_____

_____

Maxine Waters

Use a laptop, tablet or phone to access the internet and learn more about this female politician.

Age:

Place of birth:

College:

Family:

Work Place:

Record several interesting things you learned about this female politician:

 1

 2

 3

 4

SOURCES:

_____

_____

Jahana Hayes

Use a laptop, tablet or phone to access the internet and learn more about this female politician.

Age:

Place of birth:

College:

Family:

Work Place:

Record several interesting things you learned about this female politician:

SOURCES:

Andrea Jenkins

Use a laptop, tablet or phone to access the internet and learn more about this female politician.

Age:

Place of birth:

College:

Family:

Work Place:

Record several interesting things you learned about this female politician:

SOURCES:

Lucy McBath

Use a laptop, tablet or phone to access the internet and learn more about this female politician.

Age:

Place of birth:

College:

Family:

Work Place:

Record several interesting things you learned about this female politician:

1

2

3

SOURCES:

Karen Bass

Use a laptop, tablet or phone to access the internet and learn more about this female politician.

Age:

Place of birth:

College:

Family:

Work Place:

Record several interesting things you learned about this female politician:

1

2

3

4

SOURCES:

_____

_____

Loren Underwood

Use a laptop, tablet or phone to access the internet and learn more about this female politician.

Age:

Place of birth:

College:

Family:

Work Place:

Record several interesting things you learned about this female politician:

_____

_____

_____

_____

_____

_____

_____

_____

_____

SOURCES:

Carol Mosely Braun

Use a laptop, tablet or phone to access the internet and learn more about this female politician.

Age:

Place of birth:

College:

Family:

Work Place:

Record several interesting things you learned about this female politician:

SOURCES:

Eleanor Holmes Norton

Use a laptop, tablet or phone to access the internet and learn more about this female politician.

Age:

Place of birth:

College:

Family:

Work Place:

Record several interesting things you learned about this female politician:

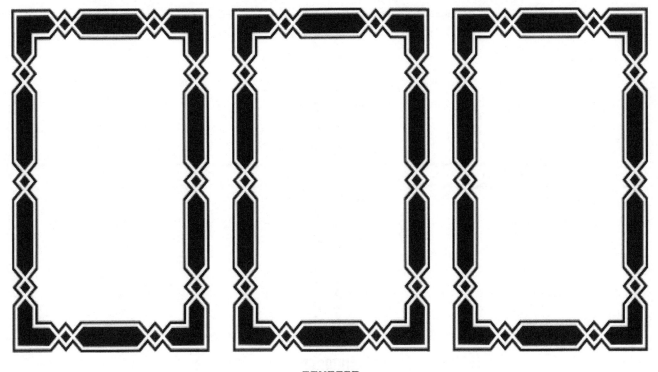

SOURCES:

_____

_____

Donna Christian Christensen

Use a laptop, tablet or phone to access the internet and learn more about this female politician.

Age:

Place of birth:

College:

Family:

Work Place:

Record several interesting things you learned about this female politician:

SOURCES:

_____

_____

Sheila Jackson Lee

Use a laptop, tablet or phone to access the internet and learn more about this female politician.

Age:

Place of birth:

College:

Family:

Work Place:

Record several interesting things you learned about this female politician:

1

2

3

4

SOURCES:

Stacey Plaskett

Use a laptop, tablet or phone to access the internet and learn more about this female politician.

Age:

Place of birth:

College:

Family:

Work Place:

Record several interesting things you learned about this female politician:

_____

_____

_____

_____

_____

_____

_____

_____

_____

_____

SOURCES:
_____
_____

Sheikh Hasini

Use a laptop, tablet or phone to access the internet and learn more about this female politician.

Age:

Place of birth:

College:

Family:

Work Place:

Record several interesting things you learned about this female politician:

_____

_____

_____

_____

_____

_____

_____

_____

_____

_____

SOURCES:

_____

_____

Tsai Ing-wen

Use a laptop, tablet or phone to access the internet and learn more about this female politician.

Age:

Place of birth:

College:

Family:

Work Place:

Record several interesting things you learned about this female politician:

1

2

3

4

SOURCES:

_____

_____

Nicola Sturgeon

Use a laptop, tablet or phone to access the internet and learn more about this female politician.

Age:

Place of birth:

College:

Family:

Work Place:

Record several interesting things you learned about this female politician:

1

2

3

4

SOURCES:

Jeannette Rankin

Use a laptop, tablet or phone to access the internet and learn more about this female politician.

Age:

Place of birth:

College:

Family:

Work Place:

Record several interesting things you learned about this female politician:

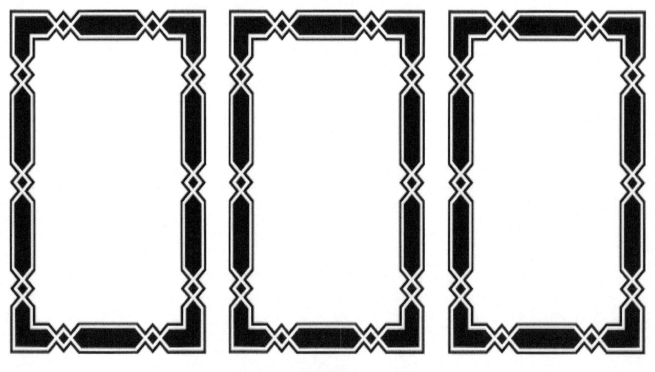

SOURCES:

_____

_____

Dalia Grybauskaite

Use a laptop, tablet or phone to access the internet and learn more about this female politician.

Age:

Place of birth:

College:

Family:

Work Place:

Record several interesting things you learned about this female politician:

SOURCES:

Erna Solberg

Use a laptop, tablet or phone to access the internet and learn more about this female politician.

Age:

Place of birth:

College:

Family:

Work Place:

Record several interesting things you learned about this female politician:

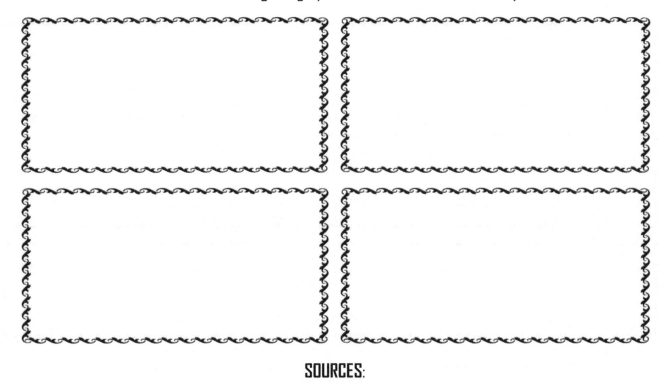

SOURCES:

_____

_____

Nikki Haley

Use a laptop, tablet or phone to access the internet and learn more about this female politician.

Age:

Place of birth:

College:

Family:

Work Place:

Record several interesting things you learned about this female politician:

1

2

3

4

SOURCES:

_____

_____

Aung San Suu Kyi

Use a laptop, tablet or phone to access the internet and learn more about this female politician.

Age:

Place of birth:

College:

Family:

Work Place:

Record several interesting things you learned about this female politician:

1

2

3

4

SOURCES:

_____

_____

Susan Collins

Use a laptop, tablet or phone to access the internet and learn more about this female politician.

Age:

Place of birth:

College:

Family:

Work Place:

Record several interesting things you learned about this female politician:

SOURCES:

Dianne Feinstein

Use a laptop, tablet or phone to access the internet and learn more about this female politician.

Age:

Place of birth:

College:

Family:

Work Place:

Record several interesting things you learned about this female politician:

1

2

3

4

SOURCES:

_____

_____

Ayanna Pressley

Use a laptop, tablet or phone to access the internet and learn more about this female politician.

Age:
Place of birth:
College:
Family:
Work Place:

Record several interesting things you learned about this female politician:

1
2
3
4

SOURCES:

Rebecca Latimer Felton

Use a laptop, tablet or phone to access the internet and learn more about this female politician.

Age:

Place of birth:

College:

Family:

Work Place:

Record several interesting things you learned about this female politician:

SOURCES:

_____

_____

Patty Murray

Use a laptop, tablet or phone to access the internet and learn more about this female politician.

Age:

Place of birth:

College:

Family:

Work Place:

Record several interesting things you learned about this female politician:

_____

_____

_____

_____

_____

_____

_____

_____

_____

SOURCES:

_____

_____

Lisa Murkowski

Use a laptop, tablet or phone to access the internet and learn more about this female politician.

Age:

Place of birth:

College:

Family:

Work Place:

Record several interesting things you learned about this female politician:

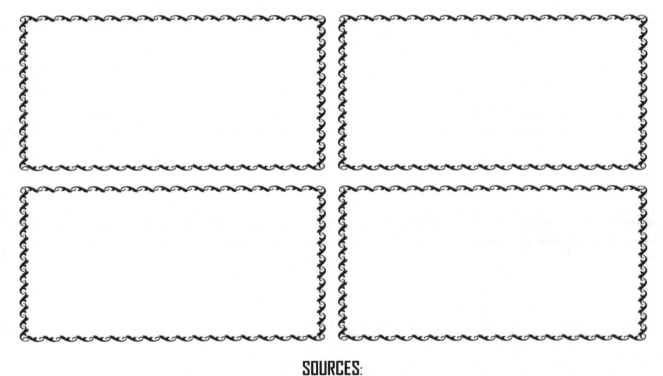

SOURCES:

_____

_____

Victoria Woodhull

Use a laptop, tablet or phone to access the internet and learn more about this female politician.

Age:

Place of birth:

College:

Family:

Work Place:

Record several interesting things you learned about this female politician:

1

2

3

4

SOURCES:

_____

_____

Jill Stein

Use a laptop, tablet or phone to access the internet and learn more about this female politician.

Age:

Place of birth:

College:

Family:

Work Place:

Record several interesting things you learned about this female politician:

1

2

3

4

SOURCES:

_____

_____

Geraldine Ferraro

Use a laptop, tablet or phone to access the internet and learn more about this female politician.

Age:

Place of birth:

College:

Family:

Work Place:

Record several interesting things you learned about this female politician:

SOURCES:

Michele Bachmann

Use a laptop, tablet or phone to access the internet and learn more about this female politician.

Age:

Place of birth:

College:

Family:

Work Place:

Record several interesting things you learned about this female politician:

1.

2.

3.

4.

SOURCES:

_____

_____

Elizabeth Dole

Use a laptop, tablet or phone to access the internet and learn more about this female politician.

Age:

Place of birth:

College:

Family:

Work Place:

Record several interesting things you learned about this female politician:

1

2

3

4

SOURCES:

Gabby Giffords

Use a laptop, tablet or phone to access the internet and learn more about this female politician.

Age:

Place of birth:

College:

Family:

Work Place:

Record several interesting things you learned about this female politician:

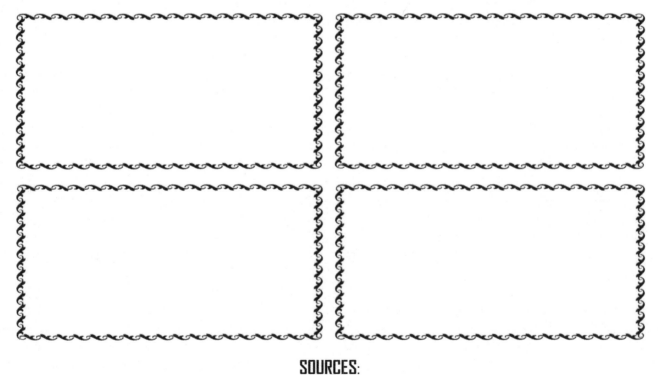

SOURCES:

_____

_____

Golda Meir

Use a laptop, tablet or phone to access the internet and learn more about this female politician.

Age:

Place of birth:

College:

Family:

Work Place:

Record several interesting things you learned about this female politician:

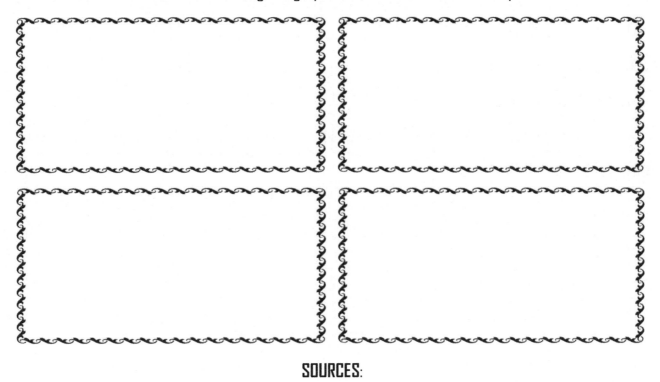

SOURCES:

_____

_____

Female Astronauts

Sally Ride, Mae Jemison, Valentina Tereshkova, Stephanie Wilson, Eileen Collins, Joan Higginbotham, Kathryn Sullivan, Shannon Lucid, Judith Resnik, Anna Lee Fisher, Margaret Rhea Seddon, Peggy Whitson, Svetlana Savitskaya, Ellen Ochoa, Kalpana Ochoa, Tracy Caldwell Dyson, Samantha Christoforetti, Christa McAuliffe, Catherine Coleman, Helen Sharman, Laurel Clark, Anousheh Ansari, Roberta Bondar, Anne McClain, Yi So-yeon, Liu Yang, Naoko Yamazaki, Sunita Williams, Nicole Stott, and Claudie Haigneré.

Sally Ride

Use a laptop, tablet or phone to access the internet and learn more about this female astronaut.

Age:

Place of birth:

College:

Family:

Specialty:

Record several interesting things you learned about this female astronaut:

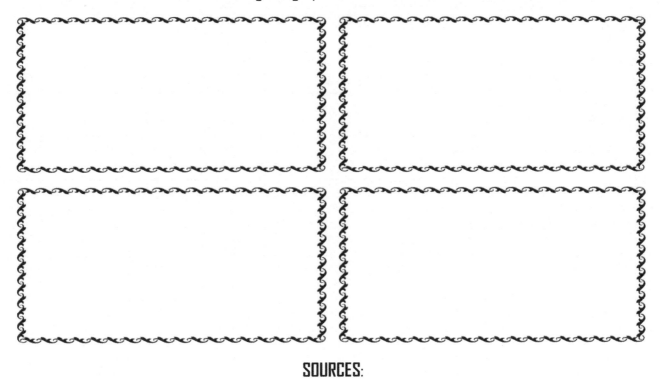

SOURCES:

_____

_____

Mae Jemison

Use a laptop, tablet or phone to access the internet and learn more about this female astronaut.

Age:

Place of birth:

College:

Family:

Specialty:

Record several interesting things you learned about this female astronaut:

1.

2.

3.

4.

SOURCES:

Valentina Tereshkova

Use a laptop, tablet or phone to access the internet and learn more about this female astronaut.

Age:

Place of birth:

College:

Family:

Specialty:

Record several interesting things you learned about this female astronaut:

1

2

3

4

SOURCES:

_____

_____

Stephanie Wilson

Use a laptop, tablet or phone to access the internet and learn more about this female astronaut.

Age:

Place of birth:

College:

Family:

Specialty:

Record several interesting things you learned about this female astronaut:

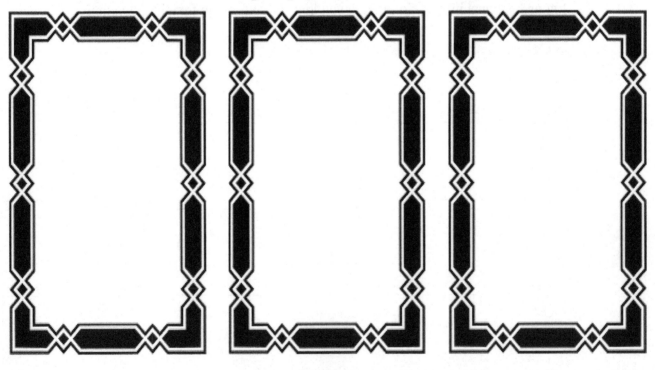

SOURCES:

_____

_____

Eileen Collins

Use a laptop, tablet or phone to access the internet and learn more about this female astronaut.

Age:

Place of birth:

College:

Family:

Specialty:

Record several interesting things you learned about this female astronaut:

SOURCES:

Joan Higginbotham

Use a laptop, tablet or phone to access the internet and learn more about this female astronaut.

Age:

Place of birth:

College:

Family:

Specialty:

Record several interesting things you learned about this female astronaut:

SOURCES:

Kathryn Sullivan

Use a laptop, tablet or phone to access the internet and learn more about this female astronaut.

Age:

Place of birth:

College:

Family:

Specialty:

Record several interesting things you learned about this female astronaut:

1

2

3

4

SOURCES:

_____

_____

Shannon Lucid

Use a laptop, tablet or phone to access the internet and learn more about this female astronaut.

Age:

Place of birth:

College:

Family:

Specialty:

Record several interesting things you learned about this female astronaut:

1

2

3

4

SOURCES:

Judith Resnik

Use a laptop, tablet or phone to access the internet and learn more about this female astronaut.

Age:

Place of birth:

College:

Family:

Specialty:

Record several interesting things you learned about this female astronaut:

SOURCES:

Anna Lee Fisher

Use a laptop, tablet or phone to access the internet and learn more about this female astronaut.

Age:

Place of birth:

College:

Family:

Specialty:

Record several interesting things you learned about this female astronaut:

1

2

3

4

SOURCES:

_____

_____

Margaret Rhea Seddon

Use a laptop, tablet or phone to access the internet and learn more about this female astronaut.

Age:

Place of birth:

College:

Family:

Specialty:

Record several interesting things you learned about this female astronaut:

_____

_____

_____

_____

_____

_____

_____

_____

_____

_____

SOURCES:

_____

_____

Peggy Whitson

Use a laptop, tablet or phone to access the internet and learn more about this female astronaut.

Age:

Place of birth:

College:

Family:

Specialty:

Record several interesting things you learned about this female astronaut:

1

2

3

4

SOURCES:

Svetlana Savitskaya

Use a laptop, tablet or phone to access the internet and learn more about this female astronaut.

Age:

Place of birth:

College:

Family:

Specialty:

Record several interesting things you learned about this female astronaut:

1.

2.

3.

4.

5.

SOURCES:

_____

_____

Ellen Ochoa

Use a laptop, tablet or phone to access the internet and learn more about this female astronaut.

Age:

Place of birth:

College:

Family:

Specialty:

Record several interesting things you learned about this female astronaut:

SOURCES:

_____

_____

Kalpana Ochoa

Use a laptop, tablet or phone to access the internet and learn more about this female astronaut.

Age:

Place of birth:

College:

Family:

Specialty:

Record several interesting things you learned about this female astronaut:

SOURCES:

Tracy Caldwell Dyson

Use a laptop, tablet or phone to access the internet and learn more about this female astronaut.

Age:

Place of birth:

College:

Family:

Specialty:

Record several interesting things you learned about this female astronaut:

SOURCES:

_____

_____

Samantha Christoforetti

Use a laptop, tablet or phone to access the internet and learn more about this female astronaut.

Age:

Place of birth:

College:

Family:

Specialty:

Record several interesting things you learned about this female astronaut:

1._____

_____

_____

SOURCE: _____

2._____

_____

_____

SOURCE: _____

3._____

_____

_____

SOURCE: _____

Christa McAuliffe

Use a laptop, tablet or phone to access the internet and learn more about this female astronaut.

Age:

Place of birth:

College:

Family:

Specialty:

Record several interesting things you learned about this female astronaut:

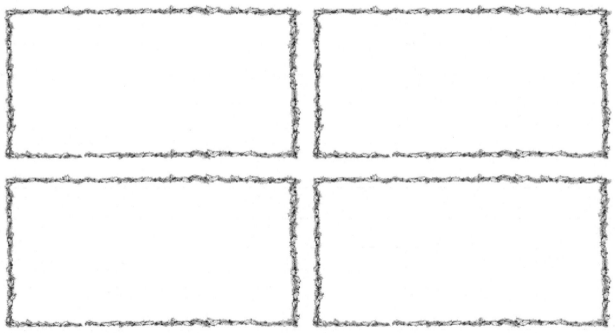

SOURCES:

_____

_____

Catherine Coleman

Use a laptop, tablet or phone to access the internet and learn more about this female astronaut.

Age:

Place of birth:

College:

Family:

Specialty:

Record several interesting things you learned about this female astronaut:

 1

 2

 3

 4

SOURCES:

_____

_____

Helen Sharman

Use a laptop, tablet or phone to access the internet and learn more about this female astronaut.

Age:

Place of birth:

College:

Family:

Specialty:

Record several interesting things you learned about this female astronaut:

SOURCES:

Laurel Clark

Use a laptop, tablet or phone to access the internet and learn more about this female astronaut.

Age:

Place of birth:

College:

Family:

Specialty:

Record several interesting things you learned about this female astronaut:

SOURCES:

Anousheh Ansari

Use a laptop, tablet or phone to access the internet and learn more about this female astronaut.

Age:

Place of birth:

College:

Family:

Specialty:

Record several interesting things you learned about this female astronaut:

1 _____
_____
_____

2 _____
_____
_____

3 _____
_____
_____

SOURCES:

_____

_____

Roberta Bondar

Use a laptop, tablet or phone to access the internet and learn more about this female astronaut.

Age:

Place of birth:

College:

Family:

Specialty:

Record several interesting things you learned about this female astronaut:

1

2

3

4

SOURCES:

Anne McClain

Use a laptop, tablet or phone to access the internet and learn more about this female astronaut.

Age:

Place of birth:

College:

Family:

Specialty:

Record several interesting things you learned about this female astronaut:

_____

_____

_____

_____

_____

_____

_____

_____

_____

SOURCES:
_____
_____

Yi So-yeon

Use a laptop, tablet or phone to access the internet and learn more about this female astronaut.

Age:

Place of birth:

College:

Family:

Specialty:

Record several interesting things you learned about this female astronaut:

SOURCES:

Liu Yang

Use a laptop, tablet or phone to access the internet and learn more about this female astronaut.

Age:

Place of birth:

College:

Family:

Specialty:

Record several interesting things you learned about this female astronaut:

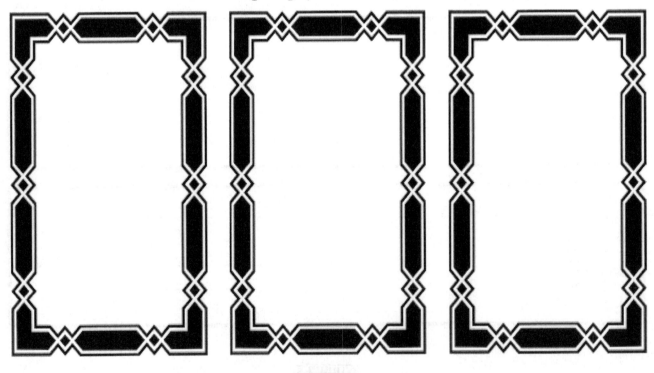

SOURCES:

_____

_____

Naoko Yamazaki

Use a laptop, tablet or phone to access the internet and learn more about this female astronaut.

Age:

Place of birth:

College:

Family:

Specialty:

Record several interesting things you learned about this female astronaut:

SOURCES:

_____

_____

Sunita Williams

Use a laptop, tablet or phone to access the internet and learn more about this female astronaut.

Age:

Place of birth:

College:

Family:

Specialty:

Record several interesting things you learned about this female astronaut:

1

2

3

4

SOURCES:

Nicole Stott

Use a laptop, tablet or phone to access the internet and learn more about this female astronaut.

Age:

Place of birth:

College:

Family:

Specialty:

Record several interesting things you learned about this female astronaut:

_____

_____

_____

_____

_____

_____

_____

_____

_____

SOURCES:

Claudie Haigneré

Use a laptop, tablet or phone to access the internet and learn more about this female astronaut.

Age:

Place of birth:

College:

Family:

Specialty:

Record several interesting things you learned about this female astronaut:

1

2

3

4

SOURCES:

Made in United States
North Haven, CT
15 March 2022